The Country Year

PAULA JOYCE

THE MEDICI SOCIETY LTD
LONDON
1984

JANUARY and FEBRUARY

1 Gladdon *Iris foetidissima.* Iris Family. Ht. to 60 cm. Flowers May to July. Another name for this plant, which grows mainly on chalk in the south of England, is Stinking Iris. The pale purple and yellow summer flowers are followed by the handsome seed-heads.

2 Winter Jasmine *Jasminum nudiflorum.* Olive Family. Ht. to 3 m. Flowers December to February. A hardy garden shrub, originally imported from China. The leaves appear later.

3 Hazel *Corylus avellana.* Hazel Family. Ht. to 6 m. Flowers January to March. In February the male catkins scatter their pollen on the tiny female scarlet flowers. The autumn nuts are a favourite with squirrels.

4 Yew *Taxus baccata.* Yew Family. Ht. to 20 m. Flowers February to April. This evergreen tree can live to a great age. It grows on well-drained soils, especially limestone, and is a common sight at the edge of woods and in churchyards. Yew wood was once used for making arrows.

5 Ash *Fraxinus excelsior.* Olive Family. Ht. to 40 m. Flowers April to May. This deciduous tree has distinctive black buds which are followed by small, inconspicuous red flowers and later by ash keys. Found in woods and grown commercially for its timber.

6 Hogweed *Heracleum sphondylium.* Carrot Family. Ht. to 3 m. Flowers April to November. The dried seed-head of this plant is one of several belonging to the same family seen throughout winter.

7 Varicoloured Bracket *Polystictus versicolor.* Width to 7 cm. This fungus lives on dead wood which it helps to rot. A common British fungus appearing in a variety of colours.

8 Clustered Feather Moss *Eurynchium confertum.* Found on shady walls, rocks and the bases of trees, mainly in the south of England. Fruits in winter.

9 Winter Aconite *Eranthis hyemalis* Buttercup Family. Ht. to 12 cm. Flowers January to March. A garden escape found in woodlands and on roadsides. One of the earliest flowers of the new year.

10 Velvet Stem *Flammulina velutipes.* Caps to 10 cm across. A common fungus found in groups on rotting deciduous trees throughout autumn and winter. The caps have a shiny wet appearance.

11 Snowdrop *Galanthus nivalis.* Daffodil Family. Ht. to 25 cm. Flowers January to March. Common names include—Fair Maids of February, Snow Princess, and White Queen.

12 Ivy *Hedera helix.* Ivy Family. Ht. to 25 m. Flowers September to November. Creeps along the ground and climbs over walls and trees. The lower leaves (illustrated here) have a more defined shape than those higher up the stem (see also March illustration).

13 Pill Woodlouse *Porcellio scaber.* Length to 12 mm. Woodlice are common in damp places throughout Britain. They feed on rotting timber and, when disturbed, roll into tight balls.

14 Ladybird *Coccinella septempunctata.* Length to 8 mm. Of the many species of red and yellow ladybirds in Britain with varying numbers of spots, the most common is the 7-spotted. Their bright colour and nasty taste dissuade birds from eating them. After hibernation, they emerge to feed on greenfly.

MARCH

1 Field Horsetail *Equisetum arvense*. Horsetail Family. Ht. to 20 cm. Common on wasteland throughout Britain, this plant belongs to a group with very ancient origins. When ripe, spores are scattered from the cone. Later in the year taller stems appear with feathery green branches.

2 Horse Chestnut *Aesculus hippocastanum*. Horse Chestnut Family. Ht. to 35 m. Flowers in May. A tall, handsome parkland tree, whose sticky buds are just starting to swell at this time of the year. The creamy-white flowers which follow are called 'candles' and in autumn shiny brown fruits known as conkers (see September and October illustration) are produced.

3 Ivy *Hedera helix*. Ivy Family. Ht. to 25 m. Flowers September to November. The upper stems (illustrated here) of this evergreen plant have a different-shaped leaf from the lower ones (illustrated on January and February page). The berries which appear late in the year and last throughout the winter are welcome food for the birds.

4 Brimstone Butterfly *Gonepteryx rhamni*. Wingspan to 58 mm. After hibernation, this butterfly is on the wing as soon as there is any warmth in the sun and is common in gardens. The male is a much brighter yellow than the female. The caterpillars eat Buckthorn.

5 Wood Dog Violet *Viola reichenbachiana*. Violet Family. Ht. to 15 cm. Flowers March to May. One of the earlier violets of the woodland. When ripe the seed pods burst open and the seeds are propelled out to be scattered by the wind.

6 Primrose *Primula vulgaris*. Primrose Family. Ht. to 20 cm. Flowers February to May. This lovely flower derives its name from Prima Rosa—the 'first rose' of spring.

7 Broad Buckler Fern *Dryopteris dilatata*. A common British fern. Illustrated here is the familiar crozier shape of the young fern frond before it unfolds.

8 Lungwort *Pulmonaria officinalis*. Borage Family. Ht. to 60 cm. Flowers March to May. A garden escape found along roadsides. The flowers start pink and then turn blue. The leaves sometimes have white blotches.

9 Lesser Celandine *Ranunculus ficaria* Buttercup Family. Ht. to 20 cm. Flowers March to May. One of the first flowers of spring. Between 8 and 12 petals to each flower. They open and close with the sun.

10 Peacock Butterfly *Inachis io*. Wingspan to 63 mm. Often hibernates in barns or sheds. Eye spots on its hind wings scare off birds. The dark underneath of the wings acts as camouflage when it rests on tree trunks. The caterpillars eat stinging nettles.

11 Coltsfoot *Tussilago farfara*. Daisy Family. Ht. to 25 cm. Flowers February to April. This is a plant of waste places. The hoof-shaped leaves appear when the flowers have died back.

12 Wood Anemone *Anemone nemorosa*. Buttercup Family. Ht. to 20 cm. Flowers March to April. These delicate flowers, which nod in the breeze on their slender stems, are commonly called Wind-flowers.

13 Lesser Periwinkle *Vinca minor*. Periwinkle Family. Ht. to 60 cm. creeping. Flowers March to May. A creeping evergreen found growing in woods and on shady banks. It is a garden escape.

1

2

3

4

5

6

7

8

9

10

11

12

13

5

APRIL

1 **Pied Shieldbug** *Sehirus bicolor.* This flying insect, one of 38 species in Britain, emerges from hibernation in the earth to feed on white dead-nettles. It is protected from predators by its unpleasant taste.

2 **Blackthorn** *Prunus spinosa.* Rose Family. Ht. to 4 m. Flowers March to April. This is a common thorny shrub growing in hedgerows or on the edge of woodland. The early blossom is followed in autumn by blue/black fruit called sloes.

3 **Common Morel** *Morchella esculenta.* A fungus found at the edges of woodland in the late spring.

4 **Great Pond Sedge** *Carex riparia.* Sedge Family. Ht. to 150 cm. Flowers April to June. Grows alongside ponds and rivers and in wet meadows.

5 **European Larch** *Larix decidua.* Pine Family. Ht. to 38 m. Flowers April. A deciduous tree, introduced into Britain, and now a familiar sight. In spring the young cones are bright pink turning first green then brown through the year. (See illustration for December).

6 **Wood Spurge** *Euphorbia amygdaloides.* Spurge Family. Ht. to 70 cm. Flowers April to June. An unusual petal-less flower. The milky-looking juice of the stem and leaves is a caustic and can burn the skin. This species of spurge is found in woods, particularly of Beech.

7 **Garden Tiger Moth Caterpillar** *Arctia caja.* Length to 45 mm. This caterpillar hibernates to emerge in spring to feed on dandelions and dock. Protected by a coat of thick hairs, it is commonly known as a woolly bear.

8 **Cowslip** *Primula veris.* Primrose Family. Ht. to 30 cm. Flowers April to June. This plant grows best on chalky hillsides. The orange spots on the petals act as guidelines for bees searching for nectar.

9 **Bluebell** *Endymion non-scriptus* Lily Family. Ht. to 50 cm. Flowers April to June. In spring these lovely wild hyacinths carpet woods, particularly of Oak. Bluebells have contractile roots—as new bulbs form on top of the soil, they are drawn down into the earth.

10 **Marsh Marigold** or **Kingcup** *Caltha palustris.* Buttercup Family. Ht. to 40 cm. Flowers March to April. A handsome plant found in water meadows.

11 **Goat Willow** or **Pussy Willow** *Salix caprea.* Willow Family. Ht. to 10 m. Flowers April to May. Male and female catkins are produced on different trees. The attractive catkins give it its name of 'pussy' willow and in spring attract butterflies and bees.

12 **Orange-Tip Butterfly** *Anthocharis cardamines.* Wingspan to 47 mm. The male of this common spring butterfly has orange wing tips, the female dark wing tips. The caterpillars eat Lady's Smock and Hedge Mustard.

13 **Lady's Smock** *Cardamine pratensis.* Cabbage Family. Ht. to 40 cm. Flowers April to June. Found in moist meadows. Flowers vary in colour from lilac to white. Also called Cuckoo Flower as it blooms when the first cuckoos are heard in springtime.

14 **Ground Ivy** *Glechoma hederacea.* Mint Family. Ht. to 40 cm. creeping. Flowers March to June. This plant with its square stem, creeps along the ground. It is not related to climbing ivy.

7

MAY (1)

1 Bladder Campion *Silene vulgaris*. Pink Family. Ht. to 60 cm. Flowers May to September. Grows along pathways and on poor grassland.

2 Emperor Moth *Saturnia pavonia*. Wingspan to 5 cm. Found on heathland, this moth is often seen flying by day. The male is smaller but brighter than the female. The eye spots dissuade birds from eating it.

3 Wood Mellick *Melica uniflora*. Grass Family. Ht. to 60 cm. Flowers May to July. Common in shady places throughout Britain.

4 Germander Speedwell *Veronica chamaedrys*. Snapdragon Family. Ht. to 30 cm. Flowers March to July. This most common of all the Speedwells grows alongside fields and roads; hence 'Speed you well' on your journey. It has hairs in two rows up its stem.

5 Cherry Gall Caused by a Gall-wasp. The Galls vary in colour from yellow to green or pink and are found in different sizes.

6 English Oak *Quercus robur*. Beech Family. Ht. to 35 m. Flowers April to May. In autumn acorns fall to the ground, many to be eaten by squirrels and other animals during the winter. Some, however, take root and by spring put forth the first new leaves of what may one day be a mighty Oak tree.

7 Flowering Cherry *Prunus sp*. Rose Family. Ht. to 15 m. Flowers April to May. Gardens and road verges up and down the country burst into blossom in springtime. One of the most popular ornamental trees is the Cherry, introduced from Japan. The blossoms range from white to deep pink and the flowers can be single or double.

8 Wall Barley *Hordeum murinum*. Grass Family. Ht. to 30 cm. Common along roadsides and on wasteland.

9 Large White Butterfly *Pieris brassicae* Wingspan to 6 cm. A common sight in gardens through spring and summer. As cabbages are a favourite food of its caterpillars, gardeners consider this butterfly a pest and call it Cabbage White.

10 Meadow Vetchling *Lathyrus pratensis*. Pea Family. Ht. to 120 cm. Flowers May to August. This plant uses its tendrils to clamber upright. Found throughout Britain in grassland.

11 Large White Caterpillar—see 9 above.

12 Buff-Tailed Bumble Bee *Bombus terrestris*. Length to 26 mm. This common bumble bee lives in large nests of several hundred. The female is slightly larger than the male. It feeds on the nectar of the Red Clover.

13 Ivy-Leaved Toadflax *Cymbalaria muralis*. Snapdragon Family. Flowers May to September. A creeping, trailing plant often found on old walls.

14 Russian Comfrey *Symphytum x uplandicum*. Borage Family. Ht. to 100 cm. Flowers May to September. This is the commonest species of comfrey. It was introduced into Britain as a forage plant and is now found in waste places and along roadsides.

1

2

3

4

5

6

7

8

9

10

11

12

13

14

9

MAY (2)

15 London Plane *Platanus x hybrida*. Plane Family. Ht. to 30 m. Flowers May. The distinctive bark flakes off leaving large creamy patches. In spring the new season's 'bobbles' hang down from the branches.

16 Cow Parsley *Anthriscus sylvestris*. Carrot Family. Ht. to 100 cm. Flowers April to June. A common sight along paths and roads. Local names include Queen Anne's Lace and Fool's Parsley.

17 Grizzled Skipper Butterfly *Pyrgus malvae*. Wingspan to 27 mm. A tiny butterfly with skipping flight, often seen in southern Britain. The caterpillars feed on Wild Strawberry, Cinquefoil and Bramble.

18 Apple Blossom *Malus domestica*. Rose Family. There are many different species of domestic apple trees and at this time of the year orchards are filled with their white and pink blossom.

19 Green Alkanet *Pentaglottis sempervirens*. Borage Family. Ht. to 90 cm. Flowers May to August. This garden escape spreads rapidly near built-up areas, alongside roads and near woods.

20 Hawthorn *Crataegus monogyna*. Rose Family. Ht. to 14 m. Flowers May to June. Spiny shrub with scented blossoms. In autumn the crimson berries, known as haws (see September and October illustration), are eaten by birds.

21 Roman Snail *Helix pomatia*. Length to 6 cm. This large British snail is found on chalky soils. It prefers cool evenings or rain.

22 Salad Burnet *Sanguisorba minor*. Rose Family. Ht. to 26 cm. Flowers May to August. Strange looking flower head with female flowers at the top and the male underneath. The illustration shows the male stage. The crushed leaves smell of cucumber.

23 Common Vetch *Vicia sativa*. Pea Family. Ht. to 45 cm. Flowers May to July. Found along pathways and in grassy places.

24 Earth Worm *Lumbricus terrestris*. While worms are a common sight we never see the many millions that are busy underground. Worms eat earth, extract the goodness and then expel the residue. The ring (as illustrated) later forms the egg case.

25 Yellow Archangel *Lamiastrum galeobdolon*. Mint Family. Ht. to 60 cm. Flowers April to July. Found in woods in central and south England. Pollinated by bees.

26 Small Tortoiseshell Butterfly *Aglais urticae*. Wingspan to 56 mm. After hibernating in sheds or barns, this butterfly emerges in spring and is a common sight on Buddleia. The caterpillars feed on stinging nettles.

27 Herb Robert *Geranium robertianum*. Geranium Family. Ht. to 45 cm. Flowers May to September. Found in shade alongside walls and wood verges. In autumn the leaves turn pink. Common names include Candlesticks from the appearance of the seed-heads.

28 Sycamore *Acer pseudoplatanus*. Maple Family. Ht. to 35 m. Flowers April to June. The hanging fruits are known as keys. When ripe in autumn, they are blown away on the wind.

29 Common Rock-Rose *Helianthemum nummularium*. Rock Rose Family. Ht. to 30 cm. sprawling. Flowers May to September. Found on chalk grassland. The petals close at night and in wet weather.

15

16

18

19

20

21

22

23

24

25

26

27

28

29

11

JUNE

1 Yorkshire Fog *Holcus lanatus*. Grass Family. Ht. to 100 cm. Flowers May to August. Common throughout Britain.

2 Elder *Sambucus nigra*. Honeysuckle Family. Ht. to 10 m. Pleasantly scented creamy white flowers are followed in autumn by black berries which are eaten by the birds. Both the flowers and fruit are used for home wine making.

3 Adonis Blue Butterfly *Lysandra bellargus*. Wingspan to 35 mm. Found on chalk and limestone downlands in the south of Britain. The male is bright blue but the female brown. The caterpillars feed on Horseshoe Vetch.

4 Common Mallow *Malva sylvestris*. Mallow Family. Ht. to 1 m. Flowers June to September. Mainly in the south of Britain along roadsides, the Latin name is used to describe the colour mauve. The fruits, which are shaped like miniature cheeses, have a nutty flavour.

5 Agrimony *Agrimonia eupatoria*. Rose Family. Ht. to 60 cm. Flowers June to September. Found growing along roads and paths at the edges of woods in the south of Britain.

6 Weeping Willow *Salix babylonica*. Willow Family. Ht. to 20 m. Flowers April to May. An introduced species often seen in parks and gardens and growing alongside water.

7 Elephant Hawk Moth *Deilephila elpenor*. Wingspan to 72 mm. A lovely coloured moth sometimes seen in an evening sipping nectar from honeysuckle. The caterpillar is said to look like an elephant's trunk—hence the name. It feeds on Rosebay Willowherb.

8 Yellow Rattle *Rhinanthus minor*. Snapdragon Family. Ht. to 50 cm. Flowers May to June. A plant, semi-parasitic on grass, widespread in Britain. Its name comes from the seed capsules which rattle when the seeds are ripe.

9 Sorrel *Rumex acetosa*. Dock Family. Ht. to 1 m. Flowers May to June. Found on grassland throughout the British Isles, this plant was once used as a vegetable.

10 Restharrow *Ononis repens*. Pea Family. Flowers June to September. A trailing plant of chalky places.

11 Large Bindweed *Calystegia sylvatica*. Bindweed Family. Ht. climbing to 3 m. Flowers June to September. Although an enemy to the gardener, this introduced plant is a lovely sight as it clambers over walls and hedges. Another name is Great Bellbine.

12 Goosegrass *Galium aparine*. Bedstraw Family. Flowers June to August. A common hedgerow plant. Another name is Cleavers as the little hooked fruits 'cleave' onto passing animals and clothing.

13 Common Wasp *Vespa vulgaris*. Wasps live in colonies and can be found in woodsheds and lofts. Their nests are made from chewed wood.

1

2

3

4

5

6

7

8

9

10

11

12

13

13

JULY (1)

1 Small-Leaved Lime. *Tilia cordata.* Lime Family. Ht. to 20 m. Flowers July. Found mainly on limestone, not so widespread as the Common Lime. The quantity of nectar it produces attracts bees and insects.

2 Teasel *Dipsacus fullonum.* Teasel Family. Ht. to 190 cm. Flowers July to August. Found throughout Britain on rough grassland and often by streams, the purple flowers attract bees and butterflies. The Teasel has many common names such as Johnny Prick Finger and Brush-and-Comb.

3 Wych Elm *Ulmus glabra.* Elm Family. Ht. to 35 m. Flowers February to March. A tree of the hedgerows which is thought to be more resistant to Dutch Elm disease. In July the winged fruits are blown away on the wind. This elm is reproduced from seed only.

4 Red Admiral Butterfly *Vanessa atalanta.* Wingspan to 72 mm. Often seen on Buddleias and on rotting fruit, this butterfly comes to Britain from Europe and North Africa. The caterpillars feed on stinging nettles.

5 Glistening Ink Cap *Coprinus micaceus.* Cap to 4 cm. This common toadstool is found on rotting wood. Like all Ink Caps, as the cap degenerates the spores form part of a black liquid mass.

6 Corn Marigold *Chrysanthemum segetum.* Daisy Family. Ht. to 45 cm. Flowers June to August. Now only rarely found growing with poppies in cornfields as they have been considered a pest by farmers since the reign of King John.

7 Field Poppy *Papaver rhoeas.* Poppy Family. Ht. to 50 cm. Flowers June to September. Sometimes cornfields filled with scarlet poppies can be seen, although this is rare. In the bud the petals are crushed tightly together, but all the creases fall out as the flower opens. The seed-head is like a tiny pepper-pot which nods to and fro in the wind scattering hundreds of tiny seeds. The poppy is seen here with a head of barley.

8 Small Copper Butterfly *Lycaena phlaeas.* Wingspan to 35 mm. To be seen flying about open ground. It has an unusually swift flight. The caterpillars feed on sorrel.

9 Wild Strawberry *Fragaria vesca.* Rose Family. Ht. to 20 cm. Flowers April to July. Commonly found along disused railway tracks and borders of woods. This plant spreads by sending out runners to form new plants. The small fruits are delicious to eat and it is the tiny pips on their surface which are the seeds.

10 Cinnabar Caterpillars and **Pupa** *Callimorpha jacobaeae.* Length: caterpillars to 32 mm. The dramatic colours of these caterpillars serve as a defence against predators. Their food plant is ragwort which as it is poisonous to cattle makes the Cinnabar popular with farmers. The caterpillars become pupae (chrysalids) before hatching out as handsome moths.

11 Cross-Leaved Heath *Erica tetralix.* Heath Family. Ht. to 40 cm. Flowers June to September. Common in bogs and moist places, the flowers of this plant vary from white to rose, and are much visited by bees. This heather grows in large clumps and is also called Bog Heath.

1

2

3

4

5

6

7

8

9

10

11

15

JULY (2)

12 Common Alder *Alnus glutinosa*. Birch Family. Ht. to 22 m. Flowers February to March. Often found alongside rivers throughout Britain. Separate male and female catkins grow on the same tree. The illustration shows this year's female catkins (green) which ripen throughout the summer until dark brown.

13 Wild Marjoram *Origanum vulgare*. Mint Family. Ht. to 60 cm. Flowers July to September. Grows on dry grassland. This plant has a strong scent and is used in cooking. In the past it was used medicinally. Attracts butterflies.

14 Sweet or **Spanish Chestnut** *Castanea sativa*. Beech Family. Ht. to 30 m. Flowers July. Mainly found in parks, this tree was introduced into Britain by the Romans. In summer the sweetly smelling male catkins grow in long racemes. (For the chestnuts, see September and October illustration.)

15 Marbled White Butterfly *Melanargia galathea*. Brown Family. Wingspan to 58 mm. This handsome butterfly is often seen on scabious and thistle. More common in the southern half of Britain. The caterpillars feed on grasses.

16 March Crane Fly *Tipula paludosa*. Length to 28 mm. One of 300 species of Crane Fly and a common sight in fields and gardens. The larvae, called Leather Jackets, feed on roots and are considered a pest by gardeners.

17 Himalayan Balsam *Impatiens glandulifera*. Balsam Family. Ht. to 200 cm. Flowers July to September. Found by streams and on damp wasteland, this tall plant may have originally escaped from gardens. A common name is Policeman's Helmet. When ripe, the seed capsules are caterpaulted away by the plant.

18 Garden Tiger Moth *Arctia caja*. Wingspan to 60 mm. This gay-coloured moth of fields and lanes is on the wing at night. Its bright colours serve as a warning to birds.

19 Spear Thistle *Cirsium vulgare*. Daisy Family. Ht. to 175 cm. Flowers July to September. Found throughout the British Isles on hillsides and alongside roads. This thistle has very prickly leaves with down on the undersides.

20 Lords & Ladies or **Wild Arum** *Arum maculatum*. Arum Family. Ht. to 45 cm. Flowers April to June. By its smell this strange flower attracts flies which become trapped at the bottom of the spathe. When the flower dies the flies escape and when visiting the next Arum transfer pollen to it. The berries illustrated here are very poisonous.

21 Privet *Ligustrum vulgare*. Olive Family. Ht. to 3 m. Flowers June to July. The wild privet is found mainly on chalk and together with the cultivated form is used for hedges. The sweetly smelling flowers blossom in July and are followed in autumn by shiny black berries.

22 Earwig *Forficula auricularia*. Length to 22 mm. After hibernation the female insect emerges in spring to lay her eggs. The earwig, which is easily recognisable by its pair of rear pincers, eats leaves, flowers, carrion and rotting fruit. Most often seen at night.

23 Creeping Jenny *Lysimachia nummularia*. Primrose Family. Flowers June to August. A creeping plant of damp places which is also grown in garden rockeries.

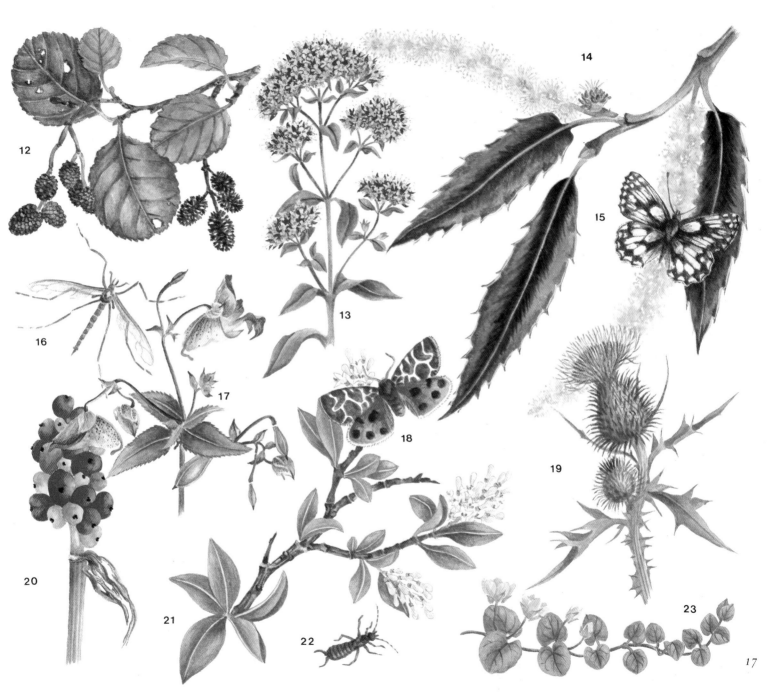

12

13

14

15

16

17

18

19

20

21

22

23

17

AUGUST

1 Sea Club-Rush *Scirpus maritimus*. Sedge Family. Ht. to 100 cm. Grows in shallow, brackish water and on mud flats. Has a triangular stem.

2 Tower Shell *Turritella communis*. Spire Shell Family. Length: 55 mm. The empty shells are often found on sandy beaches. Other names are Screw, Turret and Auger.

3 Golden Samphire *Inula crithmoides*. Daisy Family. Ht. to 80 cm. Flowers July to October. This fleshy plant is found on shingle, cliffs and salt marshes.

4 Banded Wedge Shells *Donax vittatus*. Wedge-shell Family. 25 mm across. The two separate valves illustrated here show the glossy exterior which can vary enormously in colour, and the violet interior. The live mollusc is found on sandy beaches.

5 Townsend's Cord-Grass *Spartina x townsendii*. Grass Family. Ht. to 180 cm. Flowers July to August. This grass first appeared in Southampton Water but has since spread to mud flats elsewhere in England.

6 Pod Razor Shell *Ensis siliqua*. Razor Shell Family. Empty shells of razors are often found on the seashore. Their name comes from cut-throat razors which they resemble. Razors have a muscular foot with which they quickly burrow deep into the sand.

7 Sea Lavender *Limonium vulgare*. Sea Lavender Family. Ht. to 30 cm. Flowers July to October. This plant is found on salt marshes which are sometimes carpeted with these mauve flowers which attract bees.

8 Queen Scallop Shell *Chlamys opercularis*. Scallop Family. Illustrated here is one of the two convex valves of a scallop shell. The scallop lives off-shore and when frightened moves through the water by clapping its two valves together. It is a filter feeder.

9 Sea Aster *Aster tripolium*. Daisy Family. Ht. to 50 cm. Flowers July to October. Aster means Star. This wild Michaelmas Daisy is found on muddy salt marshes and has thick leaves and stems to store water.

10 Mussel Shell *Mytilus edulis*. Mussel Family. Mussels are found grouped on rocks and piers to which they attach themselves by threads. Concentric lines show growth stages. Mussels feed on plankton. They are a favourite food of gulls and oystercatchers.

11 Bladder Wrack *Fucus vesiculosus*. Brown Algae. This seaweed grows on rocks between tide marks. At high tide bladders help keep it afloat and at low tide its slimy covering prevents it drying out.

12 Common Cockle *Cardium edule*. Cockle Family. Cockles have twin identical valves. They burrow just below the surface of sand or sandy mud on the sea shore. They are collected for food. Common.

13 Limpet Shell *Patella vulgata*. Limpet Family. Gripping tightly to rocks, limpets are a familiar sight. When covered by water at high tide, limpets move around feeding but always return to the same spot.

14 Shore Crab *Carcinus maenas*. The illustration shows a young shore crab; in adult form they are often green. Crabs have to shed their hard shells as they grow which is why so many empty shells are to be seen on the shore.

15 Sea Spurrey *Spergularia media*. Pink Family. Ht. to 20 cm. Flowers May to September. Found on muddy and sandy areas of the coasts and salt marshes.

SEPTEMBER and OCTOBER

1 Fungus *Geoglossum cookeianum*. Fungus—Earth Tongues. Ht. to 7 cm. Found occasionally in grassland in autumn especially in sandy areas.

2 Beech *Fagus sylvatica*. Beech Family. Ht. to 30 m. Flowers April to May. In autumn the leaves turn from green through gold to a lovely copper colour. Nuts are produced in quantity approximately every fourth year which is known as a 'Beech mast year'.

3 English Oak *Quercus robur*. Beech Family. Ht. to 35 m. Flowers May. Squirrels collect the ripe acorns and bury them to dig up later when food is scarce. The acorns of the English Oak grow on stalks in contrast to those of the Sessile Oak.

4 Hawthorn *Crataegus monogyna*. Rose Family. Ht. to 14 m. Flowers May to June. A common spiny shrub of the hedgerows. The scented blossom (see May illustration) is followed in autumn by crimson berries known as haws which provide food for many birds.

5 Comma Butterfly *Polygonia c-album*. Wingspan to 54 mm. An easy butterfly to recognise with its jagged wing edges and the white 'commas' on the undersides of the wings from which it takes its name. The caterpillars feed on stinging nettles and hops.

6 Sweet Chestnut *Castanea sativa*. Beech Family. Ht. to 30 m. Flowers July. Mainly found in parks, this tree was introduced into Britain by the Romans. Also known as Spanish Chestnut. In summer the sweetly smelling female flowers (see July (2) illustration) grow in long racemes to be followed in autumn by the chestnuts. These do not grow as large as those from Southern Europe which are roasted at Christmas time.

7 Hop *Humulus lupulus*. Hemp Family. A hedgerow climber carrying male and female flowers on separate plants. The illustration shows the fruit which is used in beer making.

8 Coral Spot Fungus *Nectria cinnabarina*. A common fungus on dead wood. Not edible.

9 Purging Buckthorn *Rhamnus catharticus*. Buckthorn Family. Ht. to 3 m. Flowers May to July. A deciduous shrub found on chalk. The berries must not be eaten as they have a strong purging effect—hence the name. It is the foodplant of the larva of the Brimstone Butterfly.

10 Bramble *Rubus fruticosus*. Rose Family. Ht. to 4.5 m. trailing. Flowers May to September. This plant, whose long prickly stems clamber up and over hedges and bushes, has delicious berries. The flowers of the many species vary in colour from white to pink.

11 Black Bryony *Tamus communis*. Yam Family. Flowers May to August. This plant's colourful garlands of brightly coloured berries, draped over hedges, is a common sight in autumn.

12 Horse Chestnut *Aesculus hippocastanum*. Horse Chestnut Family. Ht. to 24 m. Flowers May. A handsome tree for parks and avenues. Its springtime 'candles' of blossoms are followed in autumn by shiny brown fruits—known as conkers—enclosed in spiky green cases. (See March illustration for bud.)

NOVEMBER and DECEMBER

1 Holly *Ilex aquifolium.* Holly Family. Ht. to 12 m. Flowers April to May. The male and female flowers of this evergreen shrub appear on separate plants. The autumn berries are eaten by thrushes. It is traditional to use holly to decorate homes at Christmas time.

2 Rust (on bramble leaves) *Phragmidium violaceum.* Bramble leaves often turn dark red in autumn, but on some leaves a red blotching occurs. This is caused by a rust fungus.

3 Lichen *Hypogymnia physodes.* This lichen is found on branches and on rocks, sometimes in great masses. Lichens flourish in the damper areas of the West Country and the north, where the atmosphere is unpolluted.

4 Marble Gall Caused by the **Marble Gall Wasp** *Cynips kollari.* These tough round galls are found at the ends of Oak twigs. The gall contains only a single larva and the adult insect emerges by boring a hole.

5 Gorse, Whin or **Furze** *Ulex europaeus.* Pea Family. Ht. to 2 m. Flowers throughout the year. This prickly shrub grows in dense masses, often covering wide areas. The seed pods pop open when ripe. There is an old saying 'When gorse is out of bloom, kissing is out of season'. Even in winter it is possible to find some gorse in bloom.

6 Dog Rose Hips *Rosa canina.* Rose Family. Ht. to 3 m. Flowers June to August. These bright red berries are a common sight of the hedgerows in winter. After the frost has softened them the hips are eaten by birds. Downward curving thorns help this plant to climb high up hedges and bushes.

7 Mistletoe *Viscum album.* Mistletoe Family. Flowers June to August. Found growing on apple, lime and hawthorn trees, this parasitic plant has very ancient origins. It is now used with holly at Christmas time to decorate houses and as a 'kissing' bough.

8 Barberry *Berberis vulgaris.* Barberry Family. Ht. to 4 m. Flowers May to June. This thorny shrub was once widespread, but farmers suspected that it acted as host plant for a rust fungus which attacked their cereal crops, and so many were cut down.

9 Larch *Larix decidua.* Pine Family. Ht. to 38 m. Flowers April. Introduced from abroad, larches are now a familiar sight throughout Britain. They are deciduous. In spring the young cones are bright pink (see April illustration) turning first green then brown through the year. The cones remain on the branches during winter.

23

1. Red Campion *Silene dioica* 2. Hogweed *Heracleum sphondylium* 3. Rosebay Willowherb *Epilobium angustifolium*
4. Honesty *Lunaria biennis* 5. Bracken (frond) *Pteridium aquilinum* 6. Nipplewort *Lapsana communis*